Our Endangered Planet
RIVERS AND LAKES

Mary Hoff
and
Mary M. Rodgers

LERNER PUBLICATIONS COMPANY • MINNEAPOLIS

Thanks to Sharyn Fenwick, James E. Laib, Kerstin Coyle, Zachary Marell, and Gary Hansen for their help in preparing this book.

Words that appear in **bold** type are listed in a glossary that starts on page 60.

LIBRARY OF CONGRESS CATALOGING-IN-PUBLICATION DATA

Hoff, Mary King.
  Our endangered planet. Rivers and lakes / Mary Hoff and Mary M. Rodgers.
    p.   cm.
  Includes bibliographical references and index.
  Summary: Alerts the reader to the dangers of surface water pollution and the global imperative to keep these waters fresh.
  ISBN 0-8225-2501-1 (lib. bdg.)
  1. Water—Pollution—Juvenile literature. 2. Water—Juvenile literature. [1. Water—Pollution. 2. Pollution. 3. Water.]
I. Rodgers, Mary M. (Mary Madeline), 1954-   . II. Title.
III. Series: Our endangered plant (Minneapolis, Minn.)
TD422.H64 1991
363.73'94—dc20   90—6606
                             CIP
                             AC

Manufactured in the United States of America

1 2 3 4 5 6 7 8 9 10 00 99 98 97 96 95 94 93 92 91

Front cover: Heavy silt colors the Ikopa River, which flows through central Madagascar, an island off the eastern coast of Africa. Back cover: (Left) A young girl from Haiti, a nation in the Caribbean Sea, collects fresh water from a rushing stream. (Right) Water that soap and other chemicals have polluted swirls around a water pipe.

Recycled paper

All paper used in this book is of recycled material and may be recycled.

Recyclable

CONTENTS

INTRODUCTION
OUR ENDANGERED PLANET /5

CHAPTER ONE
THE KEY TO LIFE /7

CHAPTER TWO
LIFE IN THE WET LANE /15

CHAPTER THREE
DIRTY WATERS /23

CHAPTER FOUR
WE ARE ALL DOWNSTREAM /33

CHAPTER FIVE
ENDANGERED WATERS AROUND THE WORLD /45

CHAPTER SIX
HEALTHY RIVERS AND LAKES START WITH US! /55

ORGANIZATIONS /59

GLOSSARY /60

INDEX /63

OUR ENDANGERED PLANET

In the 1960s, astronauts first traveled beyond earth's protective atmosphere and were able to look back at our planet. What they saw was a beautiful globe, turning slowly in space. That image reminds us that our home planet has limits, for we know of no other place that can support life.

The various parts of our natural environment—including air, water, plants, and animals—are partners in making our planet a good place to live. If we endanger one element, the other partners are badly affected, too.

People throughout the world are working to protect and heal earth's environment. They recognize that making nature our ally and not our victim is the way to shape a common future. Because we have only one planet to share, its health and survival mean that we all can live.

One of earth's main elements is water. In fact, salt water and fresh water cover about three-fourths of our planet's surface. Over time, people have become more skilled in finding and using water to drink, to grow food, and to create energy. For most of these jobs, we have tapped the fresh water that is readily available in rivers and lakes.

Because the fresh water in our rivers and lakes is easy to reach, it is also easy to damage. For centuries, the amount of wastes people had put into these bodies of water was fairly small. In more recent times, the amount has grown so large that it has become a danger to the health of all living things, which need clean, fresh water to survive. By learning about rivers and lakes, we can contribute to the cleanup and preservation of this valuable resource for future generations.

CHAPTER ONE

THE KEY TO LIFE

Where would our planet be without water? We use water in just about everything we do. It quenches our thirst, keeps us clean, helps us grow and cook our food, and adds beauty and fun to our world. Water is part of nearly every manufacturing process. Water is also an essential ingredient in our own bodies. In fact, almost 70 percent of the human body is water.

Worldwide, there are 326 million cubic miles (1.4 billion cubic kilometers) of water. This huge amount covers about 70 percent of the earth's entire surface.

(Left) **Adventurous river rafters brave the rushing waters of the Chattooga River in northeastern Georgia.** *(Right)* **Farmers in the Philippine Islands of southeastern Asia plant rice in flooded fields called paddies.**

Small green islets dot the surface of Lake Nicaragua, the largest body of fresh water in Central America.

Because this water is exposed to the air, it is called **surface water.**

Most surface water lies in oceans and is too salty for human use. The remaining surface water, called **fresh water,** is largely trapped in ice. Of all the water on earth, only a tiny fraction—much less than one-tenth of 1 percent—is found in lakes and rivers. Because this fresh water is easy to reach and use, it has become very important to the many living things that share the earth.

WATER ON THE MOVE

Lakes and rivers are members of an endless circular movement called the **water cycle.** It shows how water changes form and location as it travels between the air, the land, and the ocean. Throughout the cycle, a drop of water may alter its identity many times.

To understand the water cycle, let's follow the course of a single drop of rain about to fall from a storm cloud passing over your home. When our drop hits the ground, one of several things might happen to it. If it lands on a surface that does not absorb water (such as a sidewalk), the drop might just sit there until the sun's heat **evaporates** it. Evaporation changes our drop from a liquid into a gas or vapor.

On the other hand, our drop might soak into the earth and be taken up by the roots of a plant. Plants return water to the air through their leaves in the form of vapor —an action called **transpiration.** The drop might seep far beneath the earth's surface to become **groundwater.**

If our drop does not evaporate quickly or nourish a plant or soak deeply into the earth, the water may run downhill until it enters a river or a lake. This water is known as **runoff.** From there, the drop may con-

In a Middle Eastern desert, a plant releases water through its leaves during transpiration.

tinue all the way to an ocean. The sun's heat turns some ocean water into water vapor, which moves through the air and gathers in storm clouds. Once our drop is back in the clouds, the water cycle starts all over again.

Lakes and rivers hold or carry water during its journey through the water cycle. The water they contain can come from several sources. Some water falls directly on lakes and rivers. In many cases, water comes up from below the ground to join surface water at a **discharge area.** Scientists estimate, for example, that half of the water that flows through the Mississippi River in the central United States comes from groundwater.

The most important source of water for lakes and rivers is runoff. After falling as rain, this "loose" water runs downward toward the lowest available point, usually the ocean. The runoff collects in **rivulets**—tiny, flowing channels—which eventually come together as streams. In time, as they gain volume and strength, streams form rivers. The power in the downward flow of rivers brings many of them to the ocean. Some lakes are stopping places for this water on its seaward journey.

Of course, not all water from rivers and lakes makes it to the ocean. Some lakes are dead ends, and the water's only exit is to evaporate or seep into the ground. Rivers in very hot parts of the world may dry up before they ever reach another body of water.

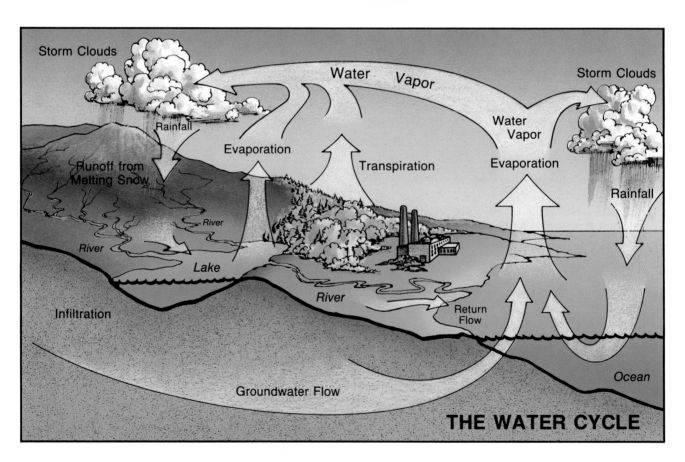

THE WATER CYCLE

Melting snow from the Canadian Rocky Mountains swells a lake in Alberta's Banff National Park.

Plenty of water completes the journey, however. Worldwide, rivers deliver about 34,000 cubic miles (141,000 cubic kilometers) of water to the oceans each year. This equals the amount of water in 1.5 trillion built-in swimming pools!

A COUPLE OF CHARACTERS

Lakes and rivers have their own unique personalities and habits. Rivers are the "pushy" members of the fresh-water family. Rarely pausing, rivers allow almost nothing to get in their way as they work to reach the sea.

A river on the island of Taiwan in eastern Asia rushes wildly over boulders on its way to the ocean.

The Grand Canyon in Arizona is just one example of the incredible power of rivers as they rush downward to meet the sea. This huge canyon formed over millions of years as the Colorado River cut through the surrounding rock along its route to the Pacific Ocean.

A waterfall is formed when a river's path takes it over a steep cliff. In Zimbabwe (a nation in southern Africa), Victoria Falls is the most forceful when rainfall swells the Zambezi River. More than a mile wide, the falls sends up smokelike mist as it crashes downward.

As rivers flow over land, they carry loose soil with them. During the last 4,500 years, the shore of the Persian Gulf in the Middle East has moved 180 miles (290 kilometers) farther out to sea. This change occurred because the Tigris and the Euphrates rivers have continuously deposited soil and rock at the place where these rivers join the gulf.

Unlike pushy rivers, lakes take life easy. They let water and soil come to them instead of gathering these materials and car-

rying them to an outlet. Much like living creatures, lakes are born, grow old, and die. Most lakes, when they are young, are fairly clear and do not hold many **nutrients.** Nutrients are chemical compounds or elements—such as oxygen, carbon, ni-

Victoria Falls forms where the powerful waters of Africa's Zambezi River fall over a cliff. A rainbow shines across the thundering falls, and a thick mist rises from the bed of the river. The name of the falls in the Bantu language is Mosiatunya, which means "the smoke that thunders."

soil and rock. Gradually, that lake becomes shallower, nutrient-rich, and full of plants. This natural aging process, called **eutrophication,** eventually may fill in the lake completely. Swamps and bogs—areas of wet, spongy ground—often form where a lake has died.

Lakes come in countless shapes and sizes. Some geographers consider Lake Superior, one of the five Great Lakes in North America, the world's largest lake. It covers the most area—31,800 square miles (82,362 square kilometers)—which is about the size of the state of South Carolina. If size is measured by volume, however, Lake Baikal in the Soviet Union is ranked first. Very narrow and more than a mile deep, Lake Baikal holds a larger amount of water than all of the Great Lakes put together!

Even though lakes and rivers are quite different, they depend on each other. Rivers feed lakes, and lakes feed rivers. On nearly every continent they work as partners, cooperating in the unending job of moving water to the sea.

trogen, and phosphorus—that living things need to grow. Scientists call deep lakes that have few nutrients **oligotrophic.**

Over time, however, the rivers that feed a lake may bring in nutrients and bits of

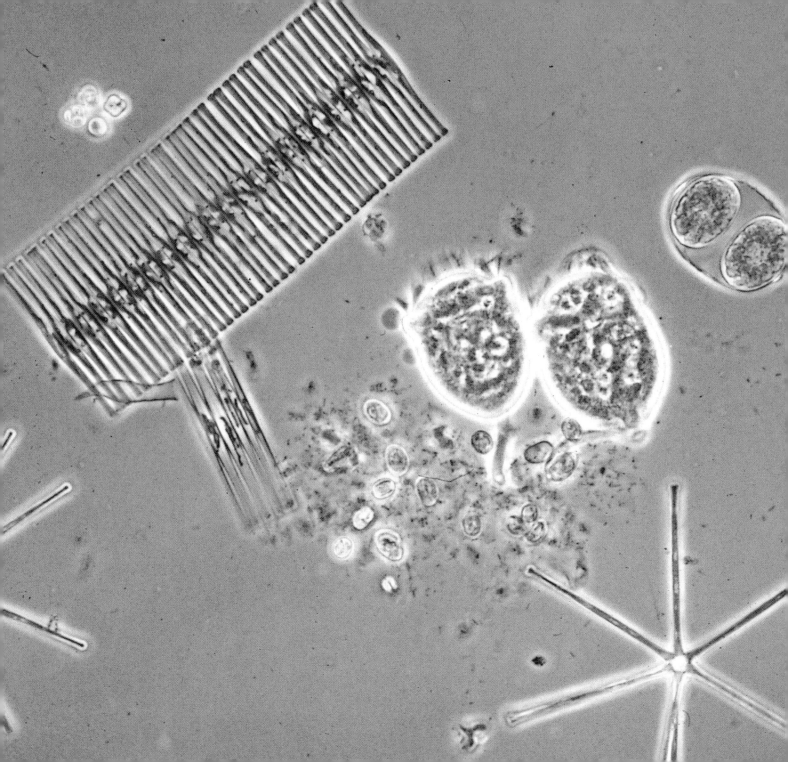

CHAPTER TWO

LIFE IN THE WET LANE

In lakes and rivers—just as in the rest of nature—plants and animals live with each other in a careful balance. Have you ever seen a drawing of a big fish that is about to swallow a smaller fish that is about to swallow a smaller fish? The drawing suggests what life is like in water, except that, in water, a lot more creatures than just fish participate.

Tiny plants and animals called **plankton** make tasty meals for larger creatures that range from insects to clams. Bigger creatures then consume the plankton-eaters. These "meals-in-a-row" are part of a complex, natural chain called a **food web.** We join the web, too, when we go fishing!

Different kinds of plants and animals live in different water conditions. Some need still water, which hardly moves, while others thrive in the rush of **rapids.** Some plankton and **algae** (tiny plants) grow well in water that contains lots of nutrients. The presence of too many nutrients, however, may make conditions unfavorable for other water life.

(Left) Plankton (very tiny animals) have been magnified many times to show the first stage of the food web. (Above) At the end of the web are people who catch and eat fish that have survived on plankton and larger creatures.

Feluccas—boats of an ancient Arab design—glide through the waters of the Nile River, which was the site of an early Egyptian civilization.

Each fresh-water organism thrives best in a certain setting. If the setting changes a lot, that particular **species,** or kind of animal or plant, may no longer be able to live and grow in the river or lake.

HISTORY'S LIFELINE

Since living things first appeared on our planet, water has been part of their **habitat,** or natural home. Some dinosaurs survived on the plants they ate in lakes and rivers. When peoples in ancient times decided to settle somewhere, they usually chose a site near fresh water.

Many past civilizations began on the shores of great rivers. The Sumerian and Babylonian cultures developed near the Tigris and Euphrates rivers. These waterways lay in Mesopotamia—a name that means "between the rivers." China's Yellow River, now called the Huang He, was the center of an ancient Asian state.

The Nile River in Africa supported the rise of the Egyptian civilization. Its people based their 365-day calendar on the Nile's annual schedule of flooding. The ancient Incan people of Peru used boats on the waterways of the Andes Mountains—including Lake Titicaca, the highest lake in the world.

Fresh surface water attracted people because of its importance in almost every part of life. People drank it and bathed in it. They traveled along the water routes and gathered food from rivers and lakes. Surface water protected towns or castles that were built on islands and shores. The water made it more difficult for invaders to attack. Rivers also provided one of the first forms of mechanical power. The flow of rivers, for example, turned waterwheels, which ran the machinery that ground wheat kernels into flour.

A THOUSAND USES

Rivers and lakes have even more jobs to do in our modern world. The biggest portion of fresh water goes to irrigate farmland. Industries require water to perform some manufacturing processes, to cool off goods and machinery, and to carry away wastes. We use water at home for drinking, cooking, and cleaning.

In the United States, these three main users—agriculture, industry, and homes—together require more than 400 billion gallons (1.5 trillion liters) of water per day. That averages out to about 1,600 gallons (6,056 liters) daily for each U.S. citizen—a quantity equal to half the water in an above-ground swimming pool.

Industries use soapy water when they loosen and clean machinery.

These same activities in other countries need greater or lesser amounts of water, depending on farming practices, on the level of **industrialization,** and on personal habits. South Americans, for example, use an average of 155 gallons (587 liters) of water per person per day for irrigation, household purposes, and industry. For the people of Africa, the amount for these activities is 121 gallons (458 liters) per person per day.

Water also plays an important part in transportation. Among the world's major "river highways" are the Volga River in Europe, the Niger and Zaire rivers in Africa, the Mississippi and the St. Lawrence rivers in North America, and the Amazon River in South America.

Hydroelectric dams harness the power of rushing rivers to make electricity. The dams are built across rivers. The water that flows through the structures turns giant wheels called turbines, which generate hydroelectric power. Almost all of the electricity in Norway, Brazil, and Uruguay comes from hydropower.

The St. Lawrence River in eastern Canada has long been a major water route. In 1759, when France and Great Britain fought for colonies in North America, British troops sailed up the St. Lawrence to battle French soldiers guarding Quebec City.

WET ENERGY
Or How Hydroelectric Power Works

People have been using water as a form of energy for thousands of years. Among the earliest hydropower machines were water-wheels, which turn when water falls on their paddles. Devices connected to the water-wheels use the turning motion as energy.

Hydropower plants now provide about 22 percent of the world's electricity. In order to produce hydroelectric power, water must flow downward in a steady stream. Hydro-electric dams hold water in an elevated lake or reservoir (place of storage), assuring that the supply is both high and constant.

As the water falls through a tunnel, it hits the blades of a huge wheel, called a turbine. The water forces the turbine to turn. A long shaft connected to the turbine drives an over-head generator, which produces electricity. Power lines from the generator carry the electricity to industries and homes. The turbine can also act as a pump, drawing water into the reservoir for reuse.

This reusable power source has its flip side. When a dam backs up water into a lake or reservoir, the land near the site is flooded. As a result, people, plants, and animals lose their habitats. Some disease-carrying insects breed especially well in the calm water on reserve. They can infect people and animals near the dam.

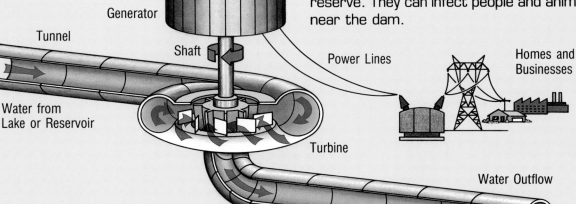

Generator

Tunnel

Shaft

Water from
Lake or Reservoir

Power Lines

Homes and
Businesses

Turbine

Water Outflow

The Madan live and fish at the junction of the Tigris and Euphrates rivers in the Middle East. These people build their homes of reeds and weave these marsh grasses into mats.

Faithful Hindus bathe in the waters of the Ganges River, which flows through northern India.

Since ancient times, people have used rivers and lakes as sources of food. In our modern world, fishing in fresh water is still an important job. For example, in Iraq, a community of people lives in the area where the Tigris and the Euphrates rivers join. These people, known as the Madan, catch fish and sell them in nearby cities.

In some countries, rivers play an important part in worship and religion. Hindus—people who follow the Hindu religion—regard many of the rivers in India, including the Ganges and the Godavari, as sacred. Believers make a ritual of bathing in the Ganges.

Water sports, such as swimming, river rafting, water skiing, and snorkeling, also draw people to lakes and rivers. Fresh water provides a habitat for many animals, such as ducks, flamingos, beavers, and hippopotamuses.

Flamingos wade in Ngorongoro Crater, a freshwater lake in central Tanzania. Created as rain filled the remains of a dead volcano, the crater attracts many species of wildlife to eastern Africa.

CHAPTER THREE

DIRTY WATERS

Found all over our planet, lakes and rivers have become a central part of life. Because they have been easy to use, they have also been easy to abuse. Many lakes and rivers have been harmed by **pollutants**—trash and chemicals that change water's natural balance. For centuries, we have treated our rivers and lakes as giant sewers for our waste.

Water pollution comes from some major and many minor sources. A huge oil spill that kills thousands of fish and a young swimmer who drops a gum wrapper in a lake are both sources of water pollution. The spill is severely damaging but does not happen often. Littering swimmers, on the other hand, may number in the millions. Let's look at some aspects of everyday life and how they can hurt our rivers and lakes.

(Left) **A polluted river in the United States bubbles with chemicals that people and industries have dumped into the waterway.** *(Above)* **A Chinese farmer allows her water buffalo to cool themselves in a stream.**

DOWN ON THE FARM

Farming to grow food is one of the oldest jobs in the world. We can live without televisions and even without socks, but we would not last long without food. Yet agriculture, in spite of its importance, also can be a big threat to lakes and rivers.

Worldwide, the main water pollutant is **sediment**—soil, silt, and other solid materials that are carried by runoff or wind from land to nearby rivers and lakes. Huge amounts of sediment wash into surface water every year. The Chang (Yangtze) River in China, for example, takes in 770 million tons (700 million metric tons) of soil annually. We would need 385 million pickup trucks to move this amount of dirt.

Although sediment can come from many sources, the runoff from farms brings large quantities of sediment into lakes and streams. Rain, snow, and wind can easily carry additional soil from unplanted farmland into waterways.

Silt, topsoil, and other materials collect in a swollen river as it flows through the central United States.

In an effort to control a flood, people in Bangladesh build reed barriers. Floods are common in this southern Asian country, where local rivers deposit their silty waters.

The amount of water that runs off land increases when large areas are cleared of vegetation to establish farms or settlements. For example, many trees in the Himalaya Mountains of southern Asia have been harvested. With fewer trees, there are fewer roots to capture the soil. It is readily picked up by rivers that flow down from the Himalayas. These waterways carry increasing amounts of soil to the land below the mountains. Bangladesh, a nation that lies below the Himalayas, has experienced severe floods as huge amounts of silty water flow into the country.

Often runoff will contain materials besides soil. Runoff can carry chemicals—such as **fertilizers** and **pesticides** that are spread on lawns and cropland—into nearby bodies of water. The risk of this kind of pollution is increasing as modern methods of agriculture are used around the globe.

On large farms, planes often spread pesticides and fertilizers over a wide area. Runoff can bring these substances to rivers and lakes.

In India, for instance, pesticide use increased nationwide from 2,200 tons (2,000 metric tons) per year in the 1950s to more than 88,000 tons (80,000 metric tons) per year in the 1980s. This is the difference between 1,100 and 44,000 truckloads of pesticides.

OFF THE ASSEMBLY LINE

Harmful chemicals, many of which end up in our lakes and streams, are part of making the things we use in our everyday lives.

Industries in the United States dump more than 250,000 tons (226,800 metric tons) of toxic (poisonous) chemicals into the nation's water each year. In Malaysia, southeastern Asia, wastes from rubber-processing plants have polluted 40 rivers, leaving few fish and mammals alive in or near them. The water in Europe's Oder River is not fit to drink because of industrial waste.

How do chemicals get from the factory to the water? In developed countries, many factories send their **waste water** (water that carries away wastes) through a **sewer system**—a maze of tunnels and pipes that empties into nearby surface water. This water may or may not be treated first to remove chemicals.

In countries that are just becoming industrialized, it is not unusual to have waste water from factories go into surface water without any treatment at all. Even water that has been treated may still contain harmful metals, such as mercury and lead.

Pollutants that leave a factory through a smokestack instead of through a water pipe can harm water, too. This kind of pollution takes a little longer to appear in water. Toxic chemicals and gases—such as lead, sulfur dioxide, and nitrogen oxide—come out of smokestacks and cling to air particles. These materials can travel many miles through the air before rain or snow carries the chemicals back to the ground, where they can pollute surface water.

A less obvious kind of pollution that some industries produce is heated water, called **thermal pollution.** Power plants that run on nuclear energy or **fossil fuels** (such as coal and oil) use water to cool the generators that make electricity. Huge quantities of water are also needed to lower the temperature of machinery and goods in many factories. This water absorbs heat from the machines.

The water used by industries and electric companies is often still too warm when

Sweden is one of the world's largest exporters of wood pulp. The factories that make the pulp have often polluted rivers and lakes with industrial wastes.

it is released into a nearby lake or river. As a result, some plants and animals die because they cannot live in heated water. In the 1980s, it was estimated that thermal pollution endangered more than one-fourth of the organisms living in surface water in the United States.

HOMEMADE POLLUTION

For most of us, water pollution is as close as our own home. If you live in a city, the water that goes down your drain or toilet probably joins water from other homes in an underground network of sanitary sewer pipes. Most of this water is cleaned in a **waste-water treatment plant,** which removes some pollutants from water before it re-enters a lake or river.

Storm sewers form another elaborate water network. They carry rainwater and a lot of other things—such as dead leaves, chemicals, **bacteria** (very tiny living organisms), and trash—into nearby rivers or lakes. In some cities, storm sewers connect with sanitary sewers, so the water from

both sources may be treated to remove pollutants. In other places, storm sewers carry rainwater and its contents directly into rivers and lakes.

In the United States alone, about 9 million tons (8.2 million metric tons) of salt are spread on highways each year. The salt melts snow and helps to keep roads safe

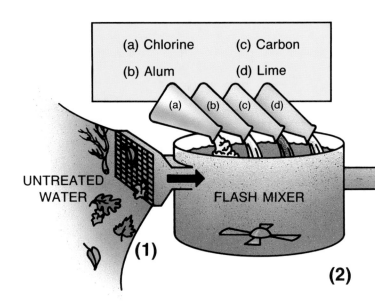

In the United States, waste water from homes and businesses collects in sewers and then goes through a treatment center before being reused. A screen

for winter driving. Much of this salt eventually washes into lakes and rivers and changes the natural chemical makeup of the water.

Huge shopping malls and other paved areas worsen the problem of urban runoff because they cover soil that might otherwise absorb the runoff. At large construc-tion sites, builders must take special care to prevent loose soil from washing off the site into lakes and rivers.

NEW FISH IN OLD WATERS

Sometimes people change the conditions in a lake or river by introducing foreign

WASTE-WATER TREATMENT

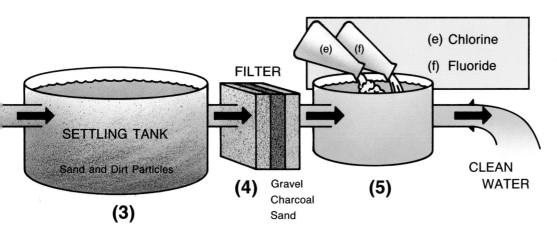

tank (3), where heavy particles of dirt and other impurities can drop to the bottom and be removed. A filter (4) takes out more impurities. The water then travels into another tank (5), where chlorine and fluoride are added to prevent new bacteria from growing. After this step, the water may be pumped into homes and businesses or it may undergo further treatment and end up in rivers and lakes.

(1) prevents leaves, sticks, and other objects from entering the treatment plant. Machines (2) mix chemicals, such as chlorine, alum, and lime, into the water to kill bacteria. The cleaned water then goes to a settling

Doubling in number about every 10 days, water hyacinths can form a thick mat on the surface of rivers and lakes. The covering takes away sunlight and oxygen from other water creatures. Water hyacinths absorb many chemicals and may have a future use as a water purifier.

plants and animals. The newcomers might be brought in on purpose—to improve sport fishing, for instance. They may arrive by accident, such as on the bottom of a boat. These new arrivals can take food and other resources that the native species need. As a result, native species can be forced out of their habitat.

Water hyacinths, for example, have taken over much of the surface water in Florida. These plants, which are native to hot, humid areas, multiply very fast. They float on the water's surface, preventing light and oxygen from getting to plants and animals below.

In the 1960s, people who wanted to improve sport and commercial fishing on Kenya's Lake Victoria introduced the Nile perch to this East African lake. Local fishermen began catching and selling the new fish. Yet many scientists are concerned that native fish species are dying out because there is now more competition for food and oxygen.

Water pollution can result from nearly anything we do. When we buy shoes or eat hamburgers or wash dishes, we have asked factories, farms, and waste-water treatment plants to use or provide water. The good news is that, since we are all part of the problem, we all can be part of the solution, too.

Women in Mali, a nation in West Africa, bathe, wash clothes, and clean dishes in the Niger River.

Water Used In An Average Day

	Gallons	Liters
To brush our teeth twice a day with the water running.	4	15
To wash our hands with the water running.	2	8
To flush a toilet takes seven gallons. We do this at least three times a day.	21	79
To take a ten-minute shower.	50	189
To wash dishes in an automatic dishwasher.	12	45
	89	336

In doing just these few tasks, we've used 89 gallons (336 liters) of water in a single day !!

CHAPTER FOUR

WE ARE ALL DOWNSTREAM

Whether big and blaring or small and secret, any action that pollutes water can harm living things. The popular saying "we are all downstream" means that what each of us does to fresh water affects someone or something else. That other person, plant, or animal may even live far away—"downstream"—from us.

Sometimes polluted water attacks our senses by making a smelly, foul-tasting, ugly mess. More often, badly polluted water changes lakes and rivers so that the creatures that normally live there cannot survive. Pollution can make the water unsafe for us to use for fishing, drinking, and

(Left) A duck tries to survive a thick covering of oil that clings to its feathers. (Right) Unless removed quickly, oil that is spilled in rivers and lakes can also threaten nearby groundwater.

playing. In some instances, polluted water can sicken or even kill people and animals who use it. Let's look at how various pollutants hurt rivers and lakes.

ALL CHOKED UP

Sediments, although not usually poisonous, can change a river by filling in its shallow spots. Another place sediments collect is at the river's **mouth**—the point where a river empties into the sea. When a lake or river becomes too shallow, some water life, such as fish and shellfish, cannot survive. Sediments coat and suffocate creatures that live on the bottom of rivers and lakes.

Very fine particles may float in the water, making it cloudy. This keeps sunlight from reaching some water plants, robbing them of the energy source they need to live and grow. The particles can also

Female sockeye salmon (far left) display a bright red color when they are ready to spawn (lay their eggs). Heavy sediments (left) can hamper these fish as they travel upstream to reproduce.

Sediments can change the types of creatures that thrive in a lake or river. In the 1800s, for example, European settlers farmed the land around Lake Ontario (the smallest of the Great Lakes) into which several rivers empty. In time, fewer and fewer salmon could live in the lake, which once was full of the fish. Salmon needed to leave the lake and swim up the rivers to spawn (lay their eggs). As soil from farmland washed into the lake, salmon had a hard time spawning. Their eggs and young often did not survive in the shallower water.

Organic wastes can include grit and leaves that flow into sewers during rainstorms.

make the water unsuitable for some fish. As parts of the food web, these plants and fish may provide nourishment to other creatures. As the food sources become more scarce, so do the larger species that live on them.

A DEMAND FOR OXYGEN

❖ Question: How are cow manure, leftover spaghetti, and a pile of leaves alike?
❖ Answer: All are **organic wastes**—wastes that contain carbon and started out as part of a plant or an animal.

When these pollutants end up in lakes and rivers, they endanger the creatures that live there. Although organic wastes might not appeal to us, they are as tasty as

Green algae (tiny plants) have begun to form on the surface of Goose River in North Dakota. Over time, the algae will block sunlight and will use up oxygen that other plants and animals need to survive.

chocolate sundaes to the bacteria and algae that survive on them.

At first glance, introducing hungry bacteria and algae might seem like a good way to get rid of organic matter. Unfortunately, during their meal, the waste-eaters also use up the oxygen molecules that occur naturally in the water around them. Oxygen is as important to fish and other water life as it is to us. When the waste-eaters rob fish and plants of oxygen, these living things die.

Because organic wastes pollute water by using up oxygen, they create what is called a **biochemical oxygen demand (BOD).** BOD is the amount of oxygen used by tiny organisms in a water sample over a specific period of time. The measure is given in the form of milligrams of oxygen per liter of water (mg/l). Environmental scientists often use BOD to show how polluted a particular body of water is.

Waste water from your house, for example, probably has a BOD of about 200 mg/l. After being cleaned at a waste-water plant, the water may have a BOD of about 25 mg/l. It may then flow back into a fresh body of water, where the treated water will mix with the fresh water. This diluting action will further lower the BOD so that the water will not harm life.

OLD BEFORE ITS TIME

Fertilizers from farms and lawns and some chemicals found in detergents can also reduce oxygen if these materials get into a lake or river. The compounds do not use up oxygen directly, but they do contain **nitrogen** and **phosphorus.** Plants need these two chemicals to grow. When nitrogen and phosphorus enter lakes, the chemicals feed algae and other water plants. When *these* fertilized plants die and sink

to the bottom, they become organic matter. As a result, there is even more food for those oxygen-hogging creatures, bacteria and algae.

Catfish—a hardy fish found in North America, South America, Europe, and Asia—can thrive in oxygen-starved waters.

The mess created by unwanted chemicals, organic wastes, and waste-eaters speeds up the natural aging of lakes. This process does not just affect plant life. Fish that thrive in clear water are replaced by other, less-desirable fish, such as carp, that can tolerate the scum and low oxygen levels.

Sometimes phosphorus causes a special kind of algae to grow that can poison animals that drink the water.

CHEMICAL SOUP

DDT…PCB…They sound like things you would find floating in a bowl of alphabet soup. In a way, they are—only that "soup" is often the water in our lakes and rivers. The letters are not harmless noodles, but short names for some of the dangerous chemicals that pollute fresh bodies of water.

Chemical pollutants can harm lakes and rivers in many ways. Depending on the chemical and its **concentration** (amount or strength), they may sicken or even kill living things. The pollutants might weaken animals, making it hard for them to reproduce. As a result, the harm that chemicals inflict may not become obvious until years later.

Some chemicals, called **carcinogens,** can cause cancer in water creatures or in the people that eat them. Other chemicals, such as salts and acids, can upset the natural balance of the water. It then becomes deadly for the plants and animals usually found there.

Bioaccumulation occurs when a fresh-water plant or animal gradually absorbs a chemical and passes it up the food web. This process can sometimes make a chemical pollutant very harmful in a body of water. Plankton, the smallest plants and animals that live in water, take in tiny amounts of a pollutant. When water-based animals eat the plankton, they absorb the chemical, too.

Since a small fish will consume lots of plankton during its lifetime, the fish ends up with a large amount of the pollutant stored in its body. Bioaccumulation continues as larger fish eat the smaller ones. Eventually, the pollutant becomes so concentrated in one animal that the contaminant can harm the next animal that eats the polluted fish.

In 1972 the U.S. government banned the pesticide **DDT** (for **dichloro-diphenyl-trichloroethane**).   DDT

RACHEL CARSON
A Courageous Voice for Change

In the 1950s and 1960s, when U.S. biologist Rachel Carson [1907–1964] was writing her books, most people did not know the words "water pollution" and "DDT." A dedicated bird-watcher, Carson noted a steady decrease in the bird populations in places that were once teeming with birds and their noise. Her study of this decline became the best-selling book *Silent Spring.*

Carson discovered that the widespread use of pesticides, including DDT, had caused the massive bird die-offs. Planes routinely sprayed these chemicals on cities and farms to rid them of pests, such as mosquitoes. Although the pesticides killed the unwanted insects, they also damaged water supplies and poisoned birds. Carson urged caution in the use of pesticides because they affected other parts of nature.

The companies that produced the chemicals criticized Carson and her book soon after it was published in 1962. But many respected scientists supported her ideas. As a direct result of *Silent Spring,* the U.S. government reviewed the nation's pesticide use. Within a decade, the United States had banned DDT. Many other countries also decided that the chemical was too harmful to use.

Silent Spring is not just about birds, however. It also reveals how the destruction of one part of nature affects other parts as well. Through her book, the general public understood the dangers of water pollution and DDT. They also saw the power of one person's voice against actions that harm the environment.

caused a lot of harm through bioaccumulation. Small creatures, such as insects and tiny fish, took in DDT. Birds that ate these animals built up high concentrations of DDT in their systems. DDT made the shells of the birds' eggs very thin, so that many eggs broke before the young could hatch. Large populations of hawks and other birds were wiped out because of DDT.

Bioaccumulation has affected our use of fish from lakes and rivers. Metals, such as lead and mercury, and toxic chemicals called **PCBs** (for **poly-chlorinated-biphenyls**) have built up in many game fish in the Mississippi River and the Great Lakes. Health agencies have warned people to limit how many fish they eat from such sources so that the diners do not also consume dangerous amounts of these pollutants.

KILLER RAIN

Sweden holds some of the most beautiful lakes in the world. The problem with many of these clear, cool lakes is that they are

A forest in Canada (above) shows signs of acid rain. It results from a mixture of rainwater and poisonous air pollutants that factories (right) and cars produce.

dead. Because of industrial wastes, these lakes contain so much acid that they no longer can support life of any kind. They are victims of **acid rain**—rain that has picked up air pollutants that occur when we burn coal and oil. The airborne pollutants, which can travel very long distances, attach to vapor as it goes through the water cycle. The pollutants combine with rain to make an acidic solution that eventually falls on lakes or reaches them through runoff.

Some lakes have a natural ability to resist acid because the rocks or soil surrounding them contain lime—a mineral that makes the acidity less harmful. But many lake-rich areas of the world are threatened, particularly Sweden, Canada, New York, Minnesota, and Norway. As industrialization spreads, acid rain is also starting to affect developing countries, such as Zambia, Malaysia, and Venezuela.

THIS WATER MAKES ME SICK!

Although many changes in lakes and rivers are dramatic, sometimes we do not notice or care about water pollution until it hits us directly. One of the most serious kinds of pollution is the presence of disease-causing bacteria or other life forms in water.

They are mainly a problem where sewage is not treated properly or where human wastes go directly into surface water. These wastes can carry the bacteria or creatures from an infected person or animal into the water. When another person drinks or washes in the water, he or she can pick up the disease.

Killer diseases, such as typhoid, cholera, and dysentery, are spread this way. The World Health Organization estimates that each day 68,500 people die from ailments carried by polluted water. In India alone, three children die *every minute* from diarrhea, a sickness often caused by drinking dirty water. The region surrounding the polluted Amu Darya and the Syr Darya rivers in the southern Soviet Union has the highest infant death rate in the country, largely because of water-borne diseases and infections.

Water pollution, then, is not just a single problem. Many different kinds of pollutants endanger our lakes and rivers and threaten the creatures—including people—that depend on these bodies of water for survival. If we want our lakes and streams, fish and birds, plants and people to be alive and healthy in the years ahead, we need to protect them from pollution.

People in many countries use untreated water from local rivers and lakes for their daily needs.

DISEASES FROM WATER

Most water used in rich, developed nations has been treated to remove the harmful life forms that cause diseases. In poorer, less-developed countries, this treatment is less common. As a result, many people in Africa, South America, and Asia suffer from water-related illnesses.

River blindness, for example, comes from water-bred blackflies. The disease causes intense itching, severe skin problems, and eventually blindness. A spraying program to eliminate blackflies in Africa has been under way since 1974. In addition, scientists have invented a drug to treat river blindness.

Guinea worm results from drinking water that contains water fleas. These fleas have eaten the unhatched eggs of guinea worms, which then settle in the human stomach and breed. Actual worms grow from the eggs, exiting the body through blisters. Guinea worm has no known cure but can be easily avoided by boiling or filtering water before drinking it.

Schistosomiasis is transmitted through contact with tiny, snail-like insects called schistosomes. They enter the body by piercing the skin. When people wade in rivers and

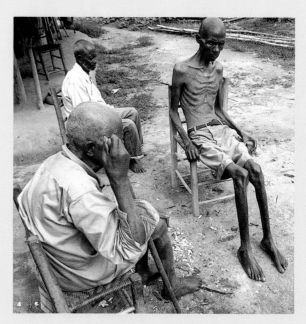

Men suffering from river blindness gather in the court-yard of their African village.

lakes to fish, collect water, bathe, or wash clothes, they can pick up the insects. Once inside the body, the insects breed, causing infections and bleeding. Killing the insects by giving victims strong drugs is effective but expensive.

CHAPTER FIVE

ENDANGERED WATERS AROUND THE WORLD

Pollution has harmed rivers and lakes throughout the world. In many places, people have seen the damage and have worked to reverse it and to prevent further harm. Let's look at how pollution has affected some lakes and rivers on our planet and at what people have done to rescue these endangered waters.

ENGLAND'S THAMES RIVER

One of the oldest water-pollution stories concerns the Thames River, a short but important waterway that runs through the heart of London, England. Flowing through a large, industrial city, the Thames was badly polluted by factories in the 1700s. Raw sewage also entered the river. Soon the

Thames was so polluted that few fish were able to live in it.

During the 1800s, the disease-infested Thames was responsible for two outbreaks of cholera that killed 14,000 people. In

(Left) Clutching a string of beads, a Nigerian gazes at the silty waters of Africa's Niger River. (Above) Many bridges—including Tower Bridge—span England's Thames River.

fact, the river was so full of toxic chemicals that when a boat sank there in 1878, many of the 600 people who died did not drown. Instead, the river's dirty water poisoned them!

A full-scale effort to bring the Thames back to life began in the 1950s. The government provided money to improve treatment of sewage that flowed into the river. Local authorities started using **aerators,** mechanical devices that mix air into oxygen-starved water. After 25 years of work and much expense, the river became a livable habitat again. Thames-watchers counted 95 kinds of fish and many species of birds in or on the river. By the 1980s, even salmon—a pollution-sensitive fish—had returned to the Thames.

Like every pollution-fighting success story, this one has a flip side. Dirty water still flows into the Thames, although not as much as in the past. Runoff from London during heavy storms floods the river with oxygen-using pollutants. Pollution-control experts send out special patrols of aerators—known locally as bubbler

barges—to fight the loss of oxygen. These experts point out that the barges do not fight other types of water pollution that still poison the Thames.

After an absence of 150 years, Atlantic salmon have returned to the renewed Thames River to reproduce.

A STINK IN RIO

Two decades ago, Lake Rodrigo de Freitas was the shame of Rio de Janeiro, Brazil. Pollution from the sewers of the crowded port city had killed the lake. From time to time, huge masses of algae grew and died, using up all the oxygen and suffocating fish. People complained about the smell. Use of the water and beaches for swimming, fishing, or playing was out of the question.

LOSING THE ARAL SEA

For thousands of years, the Amu Darya and Syr Darya rivers flowed into the Aral Sea—a large inland body of water in the southern Soviet Union. The rivers supplied 90 percent of the sea's incoming water and supported fishing and farming activities in this hot, dry region.

Since the 1920s, the Soviet government has allowed farmers to divert (take) the water from the two rivers to irrigate huge fields of cotton and rice. These crops cannot grow in the area's dry weather. By the 1960s, very little fresh water was refilling the sea. The region's hot climate was slowly evaporating the remaining water.

As a result of water diversion and evaporation, the Aral Sea is now about half the size it was in 1960. By the year 2000, the sea may cover only one-third of its former surface area. If the situation continues, scientists predict that the Aral Sea will dry up within the next 30 years.

In the late 1980s, Soviet authorities began to take threats to the Aral Sea seriously. They made plans to improve existing irrigation systems and to reduce the amount of land devoted to growing cotton and rice. These steps will prevent the sea from getting any smaller but will not restore it to its former size.

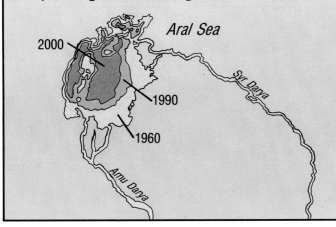

Fortunately, Brazilian environmentalists could see a beautiful lake hidden in the black mess. They set up a plan that would not only reduce the pollution going into the lake but also would clean up the damage that already had been done.

The first step was to reroute sewage so it did not flow into the lake. Workers removed the pile of solid waste that had settled on the bottom of the lake. They cleaned up the shores, planting lawns and building playgrounds in the very spots that people had once carefully avoided.

Conditions are not perfect along the shores of Lake Rodrigo de Freitas today, but they are better. People can canoe

The crowded port of Rio de Janeiro in southeastern Brazil once sent much of its urban waste into Lake Rodrigo de Freitas.

there, and plants and animals thrive in the renewed water environment. Unfortunately, cleaning up pollution takes money, and more funds are needed to finish the job. Until the lake is completely restored, the risk remains that the lake's vile smell will return to haunt the people of Rio de Janeiro.

DEATH ON THE RHINE

Until November 1, 1986, the Rhine River in central Europe had been an encouraging example of how a polluted waterway could be improved. For centuries, the towns and industries that lined the river had caused severe pollution. In the 1960s and 1970s, people began to work hard to restore the Rhine. The BOD of the river water had been reduced from 6.1 mg/l in 1970 to 2.0 mg/l by 1983. The number of animal species found in the river, which had once dropped to 25, was up to 100.

But on November 1, the river became an environmental disaster area littered with the dead bodies of all kinds of water life.

The disaster that struck the Rhine in a matter of hours began with a fire at a chemical plant in Basel, Switzerland. In the process of battling the blaze, fire fighters washed about 30 tons (27 metric tons) of deadly pesticides and **herbicides** (plant killers) into the river.

The chemicals were quickly carried downriver through France, Germany, and the Netherlands. Near the spill, almost every creature inhabiting the water was wiped out. For miles downstream, communities stopped drawing their drinking water from the Rhine to prevent poisoning people who lived along the river.

Soon after the spill, divers were sent into the river with equipment to suck the poisons from the bottom. However, the Rhine itself deserves much of the credit for the cleanup. The river's swift currents carried the pollutants rapidly downstream, diluting them and preventing them from settling in a heavy, poisonous blanket over the bottom of the river. Fish began reappearing in the Rhine at Basel in the spring of 1987.

In November 1986, workers dumped another load of dead eels from the Rhine River. The fish had washed ashore after chemicals polluted the waterway.

LIME TO THE RESCUE

It might seem odd to try to fix a polluted lake by dumping tons of white powder into it. That is just what scientists are doing to help many lakes suffering from the effects

A machine adds lime to a lake in Sweden. Scientists hope the lime will reduce the water's acid content.

of acid rain. The white powder is a chemical called **lime.**

Lime neutralizes (weakens) acid and makes water less sensitive to incoming acid rain. Pollution-control experts in Canada, Sweden, Norway, Denmark, and other areas hurt by acid rain spread lime on "dead" lakes to help them return to a more normal state. After the treatment, the experts hope that fish and plants will again be able to live in these bodies of water.

One drawback with this solution, however, is that it does not prevent more acid rain from entering the lake. Environmentalists also note that liming cannot reverse all of the chemical changes caused by acid.

THE TRUTH ABOUT WETLANDS

Movies have given **wetlands** a bad reputation. Films that show slimy, crud-covered creatures crawling out of swamps and bogs have made wetlands seem like ugly, unwanted eyesores.

The truth about wetlands is quite different. Our planet needs wetlands. These soggy areas lie between dry land and fresh surface waters. The wet, spongy soil in wetlands supports plants and animals—reeds and alligators, for example—that cannot live as well in wetter or drier environments. Wetlands also filter out harmful wastes that flow over land before they ever reach fresh water. Thus, wetlands help to prevent water pollution in rivers and lakes. They also stop floods by slowing the runoff from big storms.

People have relied on wetlands for a long time. In Ireland, many rural residents use **peat** (decayed vegetation that has become packed down in swamps and bogs) as a low-cost fuel. Farmers in Asia often plant rice in wetlands because they contain enough water to nourish the grain during its growing season. Madan Arabs live and fish in the wetlands of southern Iraq, which lie at the junction of the Tigris and Euphrates rivers.

People have also abused wetlands by draining them to create farmland. Governments and conservation groups around the world are beginning to appreciate wetlands as special habitats and as valuable pollution fighters. These vital areas—neither water nor land but related to both—now have a better reputation than they get from the movies.

Asian farmers often plant rice seedlings in wetlands, which can nourish the grain through its growing season.

AN ERIE FEELING

Have you ever been to a funeral for a body of water? People in the northeastern United States might have had the chance in the 1960s, when environmentalists mourned the death of Lake Erie.

The shallowest of North America's five Great Lakes, Lake Erie had been filling with nutrients, sediment, and organic matter from surrounding farms since the 1800s. Industrial cities—such as Cleveland and Toledo in Ohio and Buffalo in New York—grew around the lake. The people and industries in those cities routinely sent their untreated sewage and deadly chemicals into Lake Erie.

Nutrients upset the lake's natural balance of plants and animals, causing massive growth of blue-green algae. These oxygen-guzzlers gave the water a foul smell and a bad taste. Other water life could not use the algae as food. As a result, thousands of fish and plants suffocated or starved.

Runoff from farms near the lake or near rivers that fed into Lake Erie added more chemicals. In fact, one of the lake's inflowing rivers, the Cuyahoga, was so full of chemicals that it kept catching on fire. At one point, the Cuyahoga burned for eight days straight!

Lake Erie and its contributing network of rivers had been a mess for many decades. By the 1960s, the lake was dead—unable to sustain life in plant or animal form.

In the 1970s, however, a lot of people protested the decline of Lake Erie. The U.S. government provided money to build

waste-water treatment plants for the cities that lined the lakeshore. These plants sharply reduced the amount of untreated sewage going into the lake. New government rules forced factories to cut in half the industrial wastes they put into the lake between 1975 and 1981. Further reductions have taken place since then.

Gradually, Lake Erie came back to life. Fish that were brought into the lake survived. Scientists found fewer spots where oxygen was completely used up. The huge

In the 1970s, stringy, green algae covered Lake Erie (left). By the late 1980s, the lake was clean enough to permit fishing, boating, and other water sports (right).

patches of blue-green slime disappeared. People once again found Lake Erie a good place to swim and fish.

Although Lake Erie is no longer dead, it is still a long way from being healthy. Even as the water in the lake was being cleaned up, people knew that the tons of harmful chemicals had not just disappeared. They could still be found in the sediments at the bottom.

Fewer new chemicals are being dumped into the lake, but the old chemicals are still causing problems. Animals that feed at the lake's bottom stir up or absorb the chemicals of past years. As members of the food web, these contaminated animals are introducing lead, mercury, and other pollutants to the larger members of the web.

The world has many ruined lakes and rivers. Yet there are also success stories that give hope for polluted waterways. The complicated process of healing a lake or river reminds us that it is much easier to avoid polluting than to try to restore our fresh surface waters after they have been damaged.

CHAPTER SIX

HEALTHY RIVERS AND LAKES START WITH US!

Water is one of the most important ingredients of life. It is also one of the most threatened. For years, people have ignored or not believed that individuals can have an impact on our environment. Carelessly tossing a soft-drink can into a lake is an individual action. Scooping up that can and recycling it is also a personal choice. When these actions are multiplied by millions of people, the combined effort contributes to the preservation—or continued destruction—of our surface water.

(Left) A crew of young workers begins the long job of cleaning up a polluted river in rural Wisconsin. (Right) In a U.S. national park, visitors have spoiled a trail and endangered a river by failing to pack out their trash.

Here are some things all of us can do to help protect lakes and rivers.

USE WATER CAREFULLY. Each person in the United States uses up to 80 gallons (303 liters) of water a day at home. Daily U.S. water consumption is 3 times that of Japan and is more than 70 times the amount that people in Ghana, West Africa, use. All of this means that there is plenty of room for cutting back. For instance, turn off the water while you are

The recycling of aluminum cans saves most of the energy and natural resources that are needed to produce new aluminum containers.

A farmer in Ethiopia, eastern Africa, carefully waters her plants.

brushing your teeth, and take a quick shower instead of a deep bath.

REDUCE, REUSE, RECYCLE, DO WITHOUT. Think about the trash you create and help others to think about it, too. For example, when you purchase something small, avoid taking it from the store in a bag. Containers and packaging, such as plastic bottles and paper bags, create lots of garbage and do not just disappear when we throw them away.

KIDS AGAINST POLLUTION

In 1987, fifth-graders at Tenakill School in Closter, New Jersey, formed Kids Against Pollution (KAP). The students use their combined influence to change policies in their school, school district, and state that harm the environment.

One of KAP's first targets was the plastic foam (Styrofoam) that the school district used in the cafeterias. Tenakill's students knew that the Styrofoam plates, cups, and containers in cafeterias and fast-food chains are made from chemicals that destroy the ozone layer. This thin shield protects our planet from the sun's harmful rays.

The students presented the facts about plastic foam to the Closter school board, and its members agreed to stop using such containers in the district's schools. Glowing with their success, KAP then pressured its local council to pass a law to limit the use of Styrofoam. After three years of public hearings and debates, that fight was also successful.

Members of Closter's KAP have brought their concerns to people at every level of government. As one student said to politicians in Washington, D.C., "This generation is charging against the environment on my credit card." There are now hundreds of KAP chapters around the United States and in several foreign countries. For further information about starting a chapter, you can contact *Kids Against Pollution; Tenakill School; 275 High Street; Closter, New Jersey 07624.*

"SAVE THE EARTH NOT JUST FOR US BUT FOR FUTURE GENERATIONS"

*NEVER LITTER ANYWHERE—BUT ESPECIALLY NOT IN LAKES OR RIVERS.* Your trash could spell harm or death for the creatures that live in those bodies of water. For instance, many water animals have died after getting their heads stuck in the plastic rings that hold together six-packs of soda. Cut up these rings and be sure to dispose of them properly.

*BE ON THE LOOKOUT FOR LEAKY FAUCETS.* Turn them off or encourage their owners to fix them. That little drip...drip...drip uses as much as 20 percent of our fresh water supply.

Fresh-water animals often get their heads caught in plastic six-pack rings, which can squeeze the animals' throats or clamp their mouths shut, preventing feeding.

*KEEP TRASH, DEAD LEAVES, AND ANIMAL DROPPINGS OUT OF THE STREET GUTTERS.* These materials or the nutrients they contain can wash through the sewer system and reach surface water, where they eventually rob water life of oxygen.

*ADOPT A POLLUTED LAKE OR RIVER AS A SCHOOL OR CLUB PROJECT.* With your friends, collect the trash and other materials that might be fouling your adopted body of water. Find the source of the pollution and see if you can help to keep it out altogether.

*BE ENERGY-SMART.* Turn off lights, radios, and other users of electricity when you do not need them. Remember, power plants, which produce the electricity, can cause thermal pollution.

*HELP ADULTS TO THINK ABOUT CONSERVING WATER.* Remind them about the value of water if they run partial loads of laundry or leave the lawn sprinkler on all night. Urge them to consider putting in water-saving toilets and showers.

ORGANIZATIONS

AMERICAN WATER WORKS ASSOCIATION
6666 West Quincy Avenue
Denver, Colorado 80235

CLEAN WATER ACTION PROJECT
317 Pennsylvania Avenue
Washington, D.C. 20003

CONCERN, INC.
1794 Columbia Road NW
Washington, D.C. 20009

FRESHWATER FOUNDATION
P.O. Box 90
Navarre, Minnesota 55392

LEAGUE OF WOMEN VOTERS
1730 M Street NW
Washington, D.C. 20036

SOIL AND WATER CONSERVATION SOCIETY
7515 Northeast Ankeny Road
Ankeny, Iowa 50021

WATER POLLUTION CONTROL FEDERATION
601 Wythe Street
Alexandria, Virginia 22314

WORLDWATCH INSTITUTE
1776 Massachusetts Avenue NW
Washington, D.C. 20036

Photo Acknowledgments

Photographs are used courtesy of: p. 4, NASA; p. 6, Kerstin Coyle; p. 7, 25, 51, Agency for International Development; p. 8, David Mangurian; p. 9, Aramco World; p. 11 (left), p. 34 (left), Jerg Kroener; p. 11 (right), J. Padula, Maryknoll; p. 12-13, Earl Scott; p. 14, J. R. Waaland, University of Washington/BPS; p. 15, Ministère du Tourisme du Québec; p. 16, 23, Steve Feinstein; p. 17, Amoco; p. 18, Director, National Army Museum, London; p. 20, V. Southwell/The Hutchison Library; p. 21 (left), American Lutheran Church; p. 21 (right), Marty Schneider; p. 22, 26, National Association of Conservation Districts; p. 24, USDA; p. 27, Herbert Fristedt; p. 30, Florida Department of Commerce, Division of Tourism; p. 31 (left), Deborah Dyson; p. 32, 61, U.S. Fish and Wildlife, Matthew Perry; p. 33, Hans-Olaf Pfannkuch; p. 34 (right), L. Everett; p. 35, Thomas Henion; p. 36, Jeff Greenberg; p. 37, Minnesota Pollution Control Agency; p. 39 (top), Stephen Mustoe; p. 39 (bottom), Rachel Carson Council, Inc., Shirley A. Briggs, photographer; p. 40, Sierra Club of Ontario; p. 41, Husky Oil Corporation; p. 42, Sally Humphrey; p. 43, Merck & Co., Inc.; p. 44, Yosef Hadar/World Bank; p. 45, Susan Graves; p. 46, National Rivers Authority Thames Region; p. 48, Jim Cron; p. 49, DPA; p. 50, Stan Danielson; p. 52-53, James P. Barry; p. 54, 56 (right), Wisconsin Department of Natural Resources; p. 55, Kay Shaw Photography; p. 56 (left), World Bank; p. 58, Center for Marine Conservation; p. 60, Ruthi Soudack. Charts and illustrations: p. 10, 28-29, 31, 47, Bryan Liedahl; p. 19, Laura Westlund.

Front Cover: Frans Lanting
Back Cover: (left) F. Mattioli/FAO; (right) National Association of Conservation Districts

acid rain: rainfall that contains pollutants from the air. When combined with water, these pollutants form acids.

aerator (AIR-ay-ter): a machine that forces air (oxygen) into water.

algae (AL-jee): small, rootless plants that live in water.

bacteria (bak-TEER-i-yah): groups of very small organisms (micro-organisms) that eat living and dead materials.

bioaccumulation (by-o-uh-kew-mew-LAY-shun): the buildup over time of harmful substances in the tissues of animals and plants. These substances are then passed up to animals and plants higher in the food web.

biochemical oxygen demand (BOD): a measure of the oxygen used to meet the needs of micro-organisms in water.

carcinogen (car-SIN-o-jin): a substance that produces cancer.

concentration: the amount or strength of a substance within a specific space.

DDT: a modern insect killer that easily bioaccumulates in animals and plants.

discharge area: a place where groundwater joins surface water.

eutrophication (yoo-tro-fi-KAY-shun): the natural aging of a lake that occurs when it becomes full of nutrients.

evaporate: to change water from a liquid to a gas (vapor).

fertilizer: a natural or chemical substance added to the soil to help plants grow.

food web: a series of plants and animals, each of which is a source of food for the next member in the web.

fossil fuels: substances, such as coal and petroleum, that slowly developed from the remains of living things.

fresh water: inland water that contains very little salt.

groundwater: water that lies beneath the ground.

Women in Sri Lanka, an island in the Indian Ocean, bathe in a fresh body of water.

guinea worm: a disease that results from the introduction of unhatched worms into the human body.

habitat: a natural setting that provides the necessities of life for plants and animals.

herbicide: a chemical designed to kill plants, such as weeds.

hydroelectric dam: a barrier across a river that converts the power of flowing water into electrical energy.

industrialization: the introduction of modern methods of manufacturing, including machinery and a large work force.

lime: a chemical poured on lakes to reduce their acid content.

mouth: the place where a river enters the sea.

nitrogen: an element essential for plant growth.

nutrient (NOO-tree-int): a substance used as food by plants or animals.

oligotrophic (awl-i-go-TRO-fik): having a low supply of nutrients.

organic waste: waste that comes from living materials, such as plants or animals.

PCBs: a group of toxic compounds used in the manufacture of plastics.

Salmon fight vigorously—even through strong rapids—to travel upstream to lay their eggs.

pesticide (PES-ti-side): a chemical used to destroy insects or other pests.

phosphorus (FAWS-fuh-rus): an element that is essential to living things but that contributes to pollution in water.

plankton: tiny plants and animals in water that are the first links in the food web.

pollutant (po-LOOT-int): a substance that damages or ruins the natural environment and harms life.

rapids: part of a river where the current flows very fast.

river blindness: a disease carried by blackflies. When they bite a person, the flies introduce unhatched worms into the victim's body.

runoff: water from rainfall that eventually runs into a river, lake, or ocean.

schistosomiasis (shis-tuh-so-MY-ah-sis): a disease that results when snail-like insects called schistosomes enter the body and breed.

sediment: solid materials, such as soil or organic matter, that water or air have moved from their original place into a body of water.

sewer system: a network of underground pipes that directs wastes to a treatment center or other outlet.

species (SPEE-sheez): a kind or class of living thing.

storm sewers: the network of pipes into which rainwater and other materials drain after a storm.

surface water: all bodies of water whose surface is exposed to the air.

thermal pollution: pollution caused by the injection of large quantities of hot water into a lake or river.

transpiration: the movement of water through a plant's roots and leaves and out again into the air.

waste water: water that carries wastes from homes, businesses, and industries.

Wetlands play an important role in protecting rivers and lakes from pollution.

waste-water treatment plant: a place where waste water is treated with chemicals to remove or dilute pollutants before the water is returned to the environment.

water cycle: the various paths and forms that water takes as it circulates through the air to the earth and back again.

wetlands: swamps, marshes, and other low, wet areas that often border rivers and lakes.

INDEX

Abuses of rivers and lakes, 22–31, 38–43, 45–53
Acid rain, 40–41, 49–50
Aerators, 46
Africa, 12–13, 16, 18, 21, 30–31, 43–44, 56
Air pollution, 26–27, 40–41
Algae, 15, 35–38, 46, 52–53
Amu Darya River, 42, 47
Animals, 14–15, 21, 28, 32–36, 38–40, 46, 48, 50–52, 58
Aral Sea, 47
Asia, 11, 16, 24–26, 37, 42–43, 47, 51, 56, 60
Bacteria, 28–29, 35–37, 42
Baikal, Lake, 13
Bioaccumulation, 38, 40
Biochemical oxygen demand (BOD), 36–37, 48
Birds, 39–40, 46, 58
Carcinogens, 38
Carson, Rachel, 39
Chang (Yangtze) River, 24
Chemical pollutants, 25–27, 37–40, 49, 52–53
Cleanup of polluted waters, 45–54, 58
Colorado River, 12
Conservation, 51, 56–58
Cuyahoga River, 52
DDT, 38–40
Diseases and infections, waterborne, 42–43, 45–46
Electricity, 17–19, 27, 58
Endangered waters, 45–53
Erie, Lake, 52–53
Euphrates River, 12, 16, 20, 51
Europe, 18, 26–27, 37, 40, 45, 48–49
Eutrophication, 13, 37–38
Farming, 7, 17, 23–26, 35, 47, 51–52, 56
Fertilizers, 25–26, 37

Fish, 29–31, 34–35, 37–38, 40, 46–48, 52–53
Fishing, 15, 20–21, 30–31, 47
Food web, 15, 35, 38, 53
Fossil fuels, 27
Fresh water, 8, 16–17, 21
Ganges River, 21
Garbage, 55–56, 58
Grand Canyon, 12
Great Lakes, 13, 35, 40, 52–53
Habitats, 16, 19, 21, 29–31
Himalaya Mountains, 25
Home uses of water, 17, 31
Industrialization, 18, 26, 41, 45
Industrial waste, 26–28, 40–41, 52–53
Industry, 17, 40–41, 45–46, 52
Irrigation, 17, 47
Lakes, 8–10, 12–13, 15–17, 19, 21, 23–31, 33–38, 40–43, 45–46, 48–53, 55–56, 58
    abuses of, 23–31
    endangered waters worldwide, 44–53
    formation and workings of, 12–13
    protection of, 55–56, 58–59
    uses of, 15–19, 21
Lime, 50
Maps and charts, 10, 19, 28–29, 47
Middle East, 9, 12, 16, 20
Mississippi River, 9, 18, 40
Ngorongoro Crater, 21
Nicaragua, Lake, 8
Niger River, 18, 31, 44
Nile River, 16
North America, 11, 13, 18, 37, 40, 52
Nutrients in lakes, 12, 15, 52
Oceans, 8–11

Oligotrophic, 13
Organic wastes, 35–37, 52
Organizations, 59
Oxygen, 30–31, 35–37, 46, 52, 58
Pacific Ocean, 12
PCBs, 40
Persian Gulf, 12
Pesticides, 25–26, 38–40, 49
Phosphorus, 37–38
Plankton, 14–15, 38
Plants, 15, 28, 30, 34, 36–38, 50–52
Pollutants, 23–24, 26–28, 35, 37–41, 45–46,
    48–49, 52–53
Pollution, 22–53, 58–59, 62
Protecting rivers and lakes, 54–59
Rainfall, 8–9, 24, 27–28, 35, 40–41, 50
    acid rain, 40–41, 50
Recreation, 6, 21, 30, 53
Recycling, 56
Rhine River, 48–49
Rivers, 6, 8–13, 15–31, 33–40, 42–49, 51–59
    abuses of, 22–31
    endangered waters worldwide, 44–49, 52–53
    formation and workings of, 11–12
    protection of, 54–59
    uses of, 15–21
Rodrigo de Freitas, Lake, 46, 48
Runoff, 9, 24–26, 46, 52
St. Lawrence River, 18
Salmon, 34–35, 46, 61
Sediment, 24, 34–35, 52
Sewer system, 26, 28, 58
South America, 16, 18, 43, 46, 48
Species, 16, 30–31, 35

Storm sewers, 28, 35
Superior, Lake, 13
Surface water, 8, 26–28, 42, 58
Syr Darya River, 42, 47
Thames River, 45–46
Thermal pollution, 27–28, 58
Tigris River, 12, 16, 20, 51
United States, 9, 12, 17, 24, 28, 30, 38–40, 52, 56
Urban pollution, 28–29, 45–46, 52
Victoria Falls, 12–13
Wastefulness, 56, 58
Waste water, 26, 37, 42–43, 46, 48, 52
Waste-water treatment plants, 28–29, 37, 52–53
Water consumption, 17–18, 31, 56
Water cycle, 8–11
Waterfalls, 12–13
Water-related illnesses, 43, 45–46
Waterwheels, 17, 19
Wetlands, 51, 62
Zambezi River, 12–13